DEVELOPING A LOCAL CURRENCY GOVERNMENT BOND MARKET IN AN EMERGING ECONOMY AFTER COVID-19

CASE FOR THE LAO PEOPLE'S DEMOCRATIC REPUBLIC

DECEMBER 2022

ASIAN DEVELOPMENT BANK

ADB

Contents

Tables and Figures

MOF Foreword

During the coronavirus disease (COVID-19) pandemic, the economies of the Association of the Southeast Asian Nations (ASEAN) demonstrated resilience in which members have closely collaborated and cooperated in macroeconomic policy discussions to ensure the economic-financial stability in the region. Various measures were implemented to mitigate the shocks through domestics financing. The lessons from previous pandemic urged the government to raise the importance on debt management, especially the importance of local currency bond development to stimulate and support smooth economic recovery. In addition, under the global pressure particularly macroeconomic uncertainty, market volatility and tightened monetary conditions, it is critical to further enhance our own capacity by promoting the government bond market to secure the financing source for country development.

Thus, the purpose of the paper focuses on the recent development in the government bond market of the Lao People's Democratic Republic (Lao PDR) which will explore the existing challenges of the government bond issuance of Lao PDR. At the same time, it is equally significant to leverage the experiences of other ASEAN member countries. In this regard, we highly appreciate the support by the Asian Development Bank (ADB) under the Asian Bond Markets Initiative (ABMI).

The ABMI framework supports the regional financial cooperations of ASEAN Plus Three (China, Japan, and Korea). It provides knowledge sharing through forum, workshop, training, etc., also the capacity building on bond market development to pursue the objective of ABMI in promoting the local currency bond market in ASEAN+3. As the secretariat of the ABMI, ADB has played important role of sharing knowledge, expertise, and lessons from the ASEAN+3 member economies.

The analysis of this paper will not only assist the Lao PDR to develop the local currency bond market, and also potentially contribute strengthening a sustainable and resilient economic recovery.

Taking this opportunity, I would like to express my sincere appreciation to the Asian Development Bank for constructive analysis in this paper, as well as thanks to our colleagues from the Bank of Lao PDR, Lao Securities Commission Office, and also the Ministry of Finance of the Lao PDR who have been involved in providing comments and inputs on this report. Hopefully, the development of the local currency bond market of Lao PDR could be meaningful lessons to the other economies in the future.

Dr. Phouthanouphet Saysombath
Deputy Minister
Ministry of Finance
Government of the Lao People's Democratic Republic

ADB Foreword

Governments across Asia responded decisively to the economic shocks caused by the coronavirus disease (COVID-19) pandemic. However, the policy measures inevitably increased the public debt burden. Recent pressure on leading macroeconomic and fiscal indicators reveals the importance of sound public debt management and sustainable debt finance, especially through optimal utilization of the local currency bond market. Lessons from previous periods of economic and financial turbulence have shown that local currency bond markets have a critical role to play in ensuring smooth recoveries.

Deepening domestic financial markets, particularly through local currency bonds, offers diverse benefits—such as fortifying an economy to withstand shocks, while providing the government with stable sources of funding at reasonable costs, and on attractive terms of maturity. Those economies that have made progress in deepening their local currency markets are more insulated from sudden currency shocks.

The Asian Development Bank (ADB) has been supporting the development of local currency bond markets through the Asian Bond Markets Initiative (ABMI): regional financial cooperation among the Association of Southeast Asian Nations (ASEAN), with the People's Republic of China, Japan, and the Republic of Korea—ASEAN+3. The ABMI aims to strengthen the region's financial systems by developing local currency bond markets and providing technical assistance—as well as sharing members' knowledge, expertise, and experience.

This publication focuses on recent developments in the government bond market of the Lao People's Democratic Republic (Lao PDR). While this market is exposed to various challenges—many of which are shared by other developing countries—this nation can also benefit from the experiences of its ABMI neighbors. This analysis will help the Lao PDR develop a local currency bond market and promote effective debt and cash management. Nurturing a sound government bond market with realistic and transparent debt management can boost a sustainable, resilient economic recovery.

Ramesh Subramaniam
Director General
Southeast Asia Department
Asian Development Bank

Acknowledgments

This report was prepared by Satoru Yamadera, Advisor, Financial Cooperation and Integration Team, Economic Research and Regional Cooperation Department of Asian Development Bank, and Kengo Mizuno, Principal, Consulting Division, Nomura Research Institute and a consultant to the ASEAN Secretariat for the ASEAN+3 Technical Assistance Coordination Team of the Asian Bond Markets Initiative, with strong support from Emma R. Allen, Senior Country Economist, Lao Resident Mission, Southeast Asia Department.

The authors would like to express special thanks to the Ministry of Finance of the Lao PDR, Lao Securities Commission Office, Bank of the Lao PDR, International Monetary Fund, and World Bank for providing valuable comments and suggestions.

Executive Summary

This report examines the importance of the local currency (LCY) government bond market to recover from the coronavirus disease (COVID-19) pandemic. We take the Lao People's Democratic Republic (Lao PDR) as an example because the market is exposed to many challenges shared with other developing member countries. The Lao PDR can also benefit from the experiences of its neighbors in the Asian Bond Markets Initiative (ABMI): the Association of Southeast Asian Nations (ASEAN), plus the People's Republic of China, Japan, and the Republic of Korea (ASEAN+3).

Governments across Asia responded to the economic shocks caused by the COVID-19 pandemic. These policy measures, however, impacted the fiscal conditions of the developing economies. Recent pressure on leading macroeconomic and fiscal indicators reveals the importance of sound public debt management and sustainable debt finance. To manage the increasing debt burden after the pandemic, sustainable debt finance, especially through the LCY bond market, will play a more critical role.

The publication highlights the importance of (i) sound market infrastructure, (ii) enhancement of the Treasury Single Account and fiscal information disclosure, (iii) primary dealers, (iv) expansion of the investor base, and (v) coordination with collaboration among authorities and stakeholders. These are common challenges facing many emerging markets, but detailed prescriptions need to be tailor-made; so, although the Lao PDR has basic building blocks for local currency bond market development, the functionality of each block is still limited. In particular, debt and cash management need to be improved. Steps have been taken to improve the situation by establishing a Debt Management Department, and by publishing an annual bulletin with publicly guaranteed debt statistics. Our analyses provide further recommendations that can be used to develop the local currency bond market.

Abbreviations

ADB	–	Asian Development Bank
ABMI	–	Asian Bond Markets Initiative
ASEAN	–	Association of Southeast Asian Nations
ASEAN+3	–	composed of the ASEAN and the People's Republic of China, Japan, and the Republic of Korea
BCEL	–	Banque pour le Commerce Exterieur Lao Public
BOL	–	Bank of Lao
COVID-19	–	coronavirus disease
DVP	–	delivery-versus-payment
GDP	–	gross domestic product
G20	–	Group of Twenty (Argentina, Australia, Brazil, Canada, France, Germany, India, Indonesia, Italy, Japan, the Republic of Korea, Mexico, the People's Republic of China, the Russian Federation, Saudi Arabia, South Africa, Türkiye, the United Kingdom, the United States, and the European Union)
ICT	–	information communication technology
IMF	–	International Monetary Fund
LAK	–	Laotian Kip
Lao PDR	–	Lao People's Democratic Republic
LCY	–	local currency
LSCO	–	Lao Securities Commission Office
LSX	–	Lao Securities Exchange

MOF	–	Ministry of Finance
PPG	–	public and publicly guaranteed
RTGS	–	real-time gross settlement system
TSA	–	Treasury Single Account
USD	–	United States Dollar

1 Introduction

Governments across Asia responded decisively to the economic shock caused by the coronavirus disease (COVID-19) pandemic. The fiscal impact of the policy support was much more significant than that of the global financial crisis in 2009.[1] The average ratio of government debt-to-gross domestic product (GDP) rose by 9.0 percentage points in 2020 to 64.7%.[2] A sharp increase in fiscal pressures reveals the importance of sound public debt management. To manage the increasing debt burden after the COVID pandemic, sustainable debt finance, especially through the local currency (LCY) bond market, needs to play a more critical role.

This paper examines the importance of the LCY government bond market to recover from COVID-19. This publication features the Lao People's Democratic Republic (Lao PDR) as an example because its market is exposed to many challenges shared with other ADB developing member countries. This nation can also benefit from the experiences of its neighbors in the Asian Bond Markets Initiative (ABMI): the Association of Southeast Asian Nations (ASEAN), plus the People's Republic of China, Japan, and the Republic of Korea (ASEAN+3).

Section 2 explains the function of the government bond market, focusing on public finance. Section 3 describes the importance of local currency finance for debt management and debt sustainability. Section 4 explains an approach to develop the government bond market with reference to necessary building blocks and ecosystems. Section 5 describes the current government bond market situation in the Lao PDR. Following the analysis in Section 5, Section 6 identifies essential building blocks in an ecosystem, then makes recommendations for the Lao PDR, before delivering the conclusion.

---

[1] According to the *Asian Development Outlook (ADO) 2021* (using data available from 42 economies, accounting for almost 100% of developing Asia's total GDP), the aggregate fiscal deficit as a share of total GDP increased from 5.0% in 2019 to 9.8% in 2020. This is much higher than the ratio of 2.9% in 2009, during the global financial crisis.

[2] Asian Development Bank (ADB). 2021. *Asian Development Outlook 2021: Financing a Green and Inclusive Recovery*. Manila. https://www.adb.org/publications/asian-development-outlook-2021.

2 The Function of the Government Bond Market

A government bond market can play essential roles in economic development in three main ways: first, the place to finance public debts; second, the place to provide a benchmark yield and risk-free rate as a basis for various financial transactions; and third, the place to provide high-quality liquid assets.

A government bond market enables a government to raise funds from the market. Taxation is the primary source to raise funds for government activities. But flows of revenue do not necessarily match with flows of expenditure. Thus, the government needs to finance the gap to manage its cash position.

Besides, the government needs to expand spending countercyclically during periods when the economy is facing a downturn. By financing a revenue shortfall and the expansion of spending through bond issuance, the government can prevent the economy from heading into a recession, which is exactly what the governments around the world have been doing under the COVID-19 pandemic.

To finance the countercyclical measures, governments can finance locally or internationally. Issuing domestic bonds is relatively quick and easy because borrowing from international financial institutions and issuance of bonds in the offshore market involves a negotiation. It is also necessary to note that offshore bond issuance usually requires a country rating, which may worsen when the country is facing an economic challenge. In principle, the issuance of debts does not necessarily affect a country's rating because a rating should reflect creditworthiness through the economic cycles. But debt affordability, a ratio of interest payment against revenue, which would inevitably arise during economic difficulty, tends to translate into lower ratings.[3] Therefore, foreign borrowing may require additional careful consideration compared to domestic bond issuance—whose credit rating is usually the highest in a domestic market, hence its funding costs are the lowest.

Governments can also issue bonds to share the costs of financing public infrastructures across generations. If it is assumed that the average lifespan of infrastructures is 50 years, debts to finance the infrastructures should be repaid over 50 years. The repayment burdens and benefits from infrastructures can be shared across generations from the viewpoint of intergenerational equity. If the cost of infrastructures has to be shouldered entirely by the current generation, infrastructures would be undersupplied. Therefore, to ensure intergenerational equity and avoid underserving infrastructure investments, the government needs to consider financing by issuing long-term bonds.

So far, the government measures against the COVID-19 pandemic are focused on containment and sustainment. But the measures will need to shift to prevention, disaster reduction, and economic resilience and strength to support a more resilient recovery. They would require a long-term strategy and long-term investment. Particularly, the recovery should apply new technologies and innovations and accelerate digital transformation by making

---

[3]   M. Amstad and F. Packer. 2015. Sovereign Ratings of Advanced and Emerging Economies After the Crisis. *BIS Quarterly Review*. December. Basel.

adequate investments in information and communication technology (ICT) to be inclusive and equitable.[4] Empirical findings by the *Asian Development Outlook (ADO) 2021* show countries with better ICT infrastructure have been more successful in cushioning the economic shock of COVID-19 by shifting more activities online.[2] The economies with underdeveloped ICT infrastructure must invest more to make them resilient and accelerate their recovery.

Although developing Asia previously managed to sustain relatively low debt levels, this may not be achievable again in the near future. The International Monetary Fund (IMF) estimates, up to 2025, low-income countries would require an additional USD200 billion to step up the response to COVID-19 and build adequate financial buffers.[5] To finance and support a more resilient recovery, debt management needs to be improved. Strategic fiscal planning, enhanced fiscal transparency, and better communication with the market would ensure market confidence and credibility; hence, additional debts would be absorbed smoothly as credible assets and translated to higher market liquidity.

[4]   ADB. 2021. *Disaster Resilience in Asia*. Manila.
[5]   International Monetary Fund (IMF). 2021. Macroeconomic Developments and Prospects In Low-Income Countries—2021. *Policy Paper*. No. 2021/020. Washington, DC.

3 Importance of Local Currency Finance for Debt Management and Sustainability

To manage government debts sustainably, it is vital to develop an LCY bond market. The 1997–1998 Asian financial crisis highlighted that the lack of a domestic bond market would cause major financial risks. So-called double mismatches, mismatches in currency and maturity, were identified as one of the root causes of the crisis. Since then, ASEAN+3 has been promoting the development of local currency bond markets under the ABMI in the region.

Since the establishment of the ABMI, the five original members of the Association of Southeast Asian Nations (ASEAN), namely, Indonesia, Malaysia, the Philippines, Singapore, and Thailand, plus the PRC, the Republic of Korea, and Viet Nam have achieved remarkable progress in developing their respective domestic bond markets (Figure 1). Particularly, thanks to the significant growth of the PRC, the total size of the markets is now comparable to the United States (US) Treasury debts.

Figure 1: Local Currency Bonds Outstanding

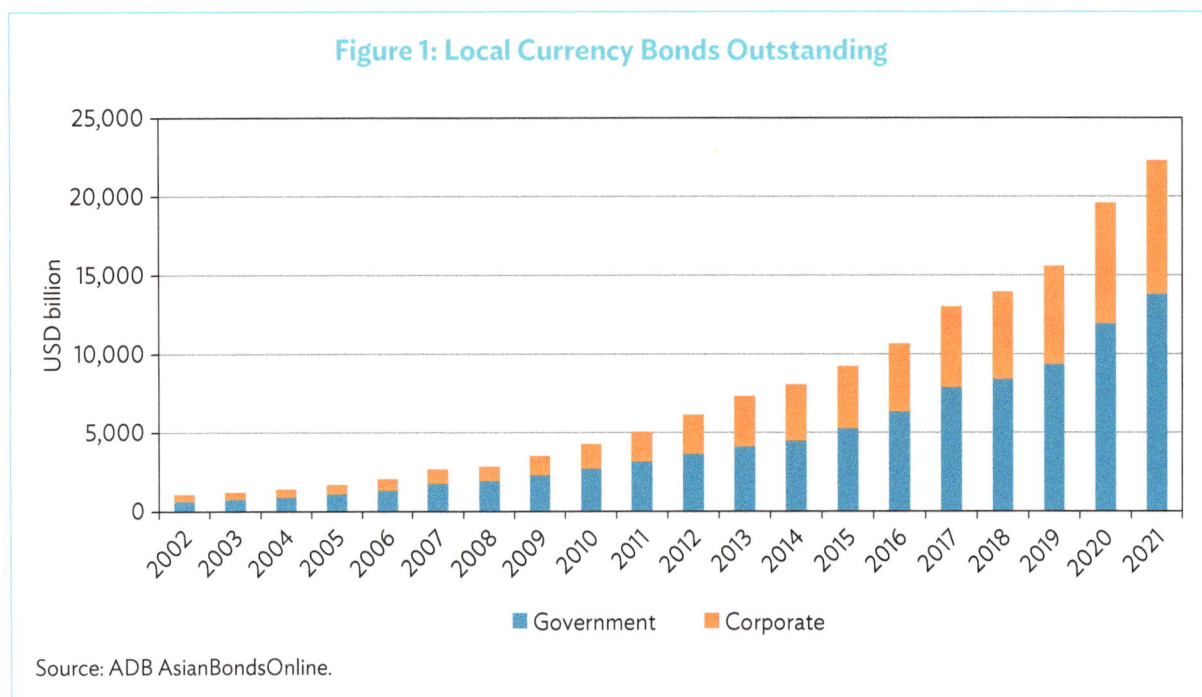

Source: ADB AsianBondsOnline.

The global financial crisis in 2007–2008 also made us realize again the importance of an LCY bond market. In 2011, the Group of Twenty (G20) launched an initiative at the G20 Cannes Summit to develop LCY bond markets. The G20 recognized that a well-developed LCY bond market (i) increases a country's ability to withstand global capital flows; (ii) reduces its reliance on foreign currency borrowing and lessens exchange rate risks; (iii) contributes to the reduction of current account imbalances; (iv) lowers the need for large precautionary reserve holdings; and (v) allows bank and corporate balance sheets to adjust more smoothly, hence, improving the capacity of macroeconomic policies to respond to external shocks.[6]

By mobilizing domestic savings, a domestic bond market can reduce negative spillovers from weaknesses in the banking sector including the impact of global financial stress through the banking sector. According to Valendia-Rubiano, Silva, and Anderson (2010), the countries with larger and more developed domestic bond markets were less affected by the global financial crisis.[7] Park, Shin, and Tian (2018) also examined the financial vulnerability of developing countries during the global financial crisis and the taper tantrum in 2013 and found a negative association between the growth of LCY bond markets and the degree of currency depreciation in emerging economies.[8] LCY bond markets with a high share of domestic investors and reasonable macroeconomic stability have been proven to be more immune to volatile capital flows.[9]

---

[6]   IMF and World Bank. 2018. Staff note for the G20 International Financial Architecture Working Group (IFAWG) recent developments on local currency bond markets in emerging economies. Washington, DC.

[7]   A. Valendia-Rubiano, A. C. Silva, and P. R. D. Anderson. 2010. Public Debt Management in Emerging Market Economies. *World Bank Policy Research Working Paper.* No. 5399. Washington, DC.

[8]   D. Park, K. Shin, and S. Tian. 2018. Do Local Currency Bond Markets Enhance Financial Stability? *ADB Economic Working Paper Series.* No. 563. Manila.

[9]   IMF and World Bank. 2016. Development of Local Currency Bond Markets Overview of Recent Developments and Key Themes. *Staff Note for the G20 IFAWG.* Seoul.

4 Necessary Building Blocks and Ecosystems to Develop a Government Bond Market

To develop a bond market, relevant institutions must act as its building blocks. In addition, ecosystems to ensure the functionality of the market must be developed.[10] The relevant stakeholders and necessary building blocks for a government bond market are: (i) the ministry of finance as a government bond issuer; (ii) the central bank as a fiscal agent, registrar for government bonds, and market participant conducting monetary operations in the bond and money markets; (iii) the securities market regulator as the guardian of market integrity; (iv) primary dealers who underwrite government bonds; (v) investors, particularly institutional investors such as banks, insurance companies, and pension funds; (vi) intermediaries in secondary markets such as brokers, dealers, and price information providers; (vii) organized markets to provide a trading place and a fair price-finding mechanism; and (viii) securities settlement and safekeeping infrastructure to ensure the smooth fulfillment of transactions and asset safety.

Besides, it is necessary to consider interactions among these building blocks and the enabling environment as ecosystems that support the function and integrity of the market (Figure 2). To build and maintain an efficient bond market, first, it is necessary to have a comprehensive and robust legal framework in place. Second, the availability of information and market transparency also supports bond market development. Particularly, for the government bond market development, the government should disclose its fiscal conditions, share its debt management policy and strategy, and announce an issuance schedule regularly in advance to market participants. Third, to create transactions in a bond market, information on bond prices is necessary to match demand and supply. Since the government bond yields are seen as the benchmark rates for various financial transactions, the price information needs to be open and reliable. Fourth, safe and efficient trade, payment, clearing, and settlement systems must be in place. Since the value of government

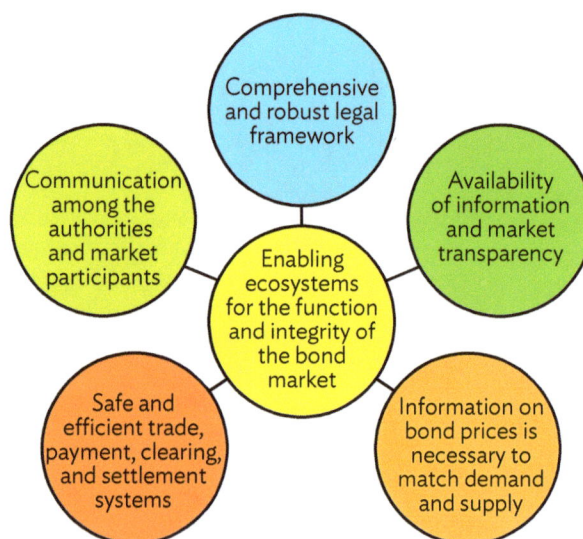

Figure 2: Ecosystems for an Efficient Government Bond Market

Source: Author's schematization.

bond transactions is large, a settlement risk must be avoided as much as possible. Besides, system linkage and coordination need to be considered to reduce systemic risk. Last, smooth communication among the authorities

---

10 ADB. 2019. *Good Practices for Developing a Local Currency Bond Market: Lessons from the ASEAN+3 Asian Bond Markets Initiative.* Manila.

and communication with market participants should be established. Especially, communication between the government as an issuer and market participants is very important in developing the market.

Based on the individual experiences of ASEAN+3 member economies, there is no one-size-fits-all approach to the development of a bond market. The level of market development, institutional arrangement, and readiness would vary depending on the market. Thus, it would not be practical to apply the same prescriptions to all. Careful diagnostics must be made before applying possible policy actions.

5 Overview of the Lao PDR Government Bond Market

Like the other countries, the fiscal condition of the Lao PDR has deteriorated due to the COVID-19 pandemic. The Lao PDR needs more attention because the size of public and publicly guaranteed (PPG) debt to its economy is larger compared to the neighboring countries (Table 1). Besides, the ratio of its external debts is higher (Table 2). The Lao PDR may be affected more by foreign exchange movements. As a lesson from the Asian financial crisis, a huge currency mismatch is a potential source of a crisis. It is urgent for the Lao PDR to develop its government bond market further to reduce its reliance on external debts as much as possible.

Table 1: Government Gross Debt-to-GDP Ratio in Select ASEAN Member States

ASEAN Member States	2018	2019	2020	2021
Cambodia	28.50%	28.60%	34.30%	38.70%
Lao PDR	59.70%	62.00%	82.60%	95.20%
Thailand	41.90%	41.10%	49.80%	58.00%
Viet Nam	43.70%	41.30%	41.70%	40.20%

Lao PDR = Lao People's Democratic Republic.
Source: IMF. 2022. *Fiscal Monitor: Fiscal Policy from Pandemic to War*. April.

Table 2: External and Domestic Proportions of PPG Debt Outstanding

ASEAN Member States	External	Domestic
Cambodia (2021 Q4)	100%	0%
Lao PDR (2021 Q4)	86%	14%
Thailand (2022 Q1)	2%	98%
Viet Nam (2021 Q2)	36%	64%

Lao PDR = Lao Paople's Democratic Republic, MOF = Ministry of Finance, PPG = public and publicly guaranteed, Q = quarter.

Sources: Cambodia MEF, *Public Debt Statistical Bulletin 2021*; Lao MOF, *Annual PPG Debt Statistics Bulletin 2021*; Thailand MOF website; Viet Nam MOF, *Public Debt Bulletin 2017-6/2021*.

The bond market of the Lao PDR was created in 1994 when Treasury bills were issued for the first time to help finance the annual budget deficit. Since then, government securities have been issued regularly to finance the budget deficit and to repay public debts.

5.1 Legal and Regulatory Framework of the Lao PDR Government Bond Market

As a necessary ecosystem for government bond market development, the legal and regulatory framework for public debt management should clarify the responsibilities of debt management policy, primary debt issues, secondary market arrangements, depository facilities, and clearing and settlement arrangements for trading.

In the Lao PDR, the Ministry of Finance (MOF), the Bank of Lao (BOL), and the Lao Securities Commission Office (LSCO) under the BOL are the policy bodies and regulatory authorities that govern the government bond market. The MOF is the issuer of the government securities, and the BOL can act as an agent for the government in relation to the government bond issuance and regulates banks that are the biggest investors of the government securities. The LSCO regulates the securities market, including government securities listed on the Lao Securities Exchange (LSX). The total amount of government securities issued in 1 year is set by the annual state budget plan adopted by the National Assembly.

The Law on State Budget stipulates the procedures for preparing and adopting annual state budget plans, which include the issuance and repayment of government securities as a part of domestic financing. The Law on Public Debt Management stipulates issuance forms, methods, procedures, and types of government securities. The Law on Bank of Lao PDR stipulates distribution, sell, buy, and settlement of government bond administrations as one of the functions of the BOL. The Law on Securities stipulates depository and listing of government securities issued through the securities market, which are currently the functions of the LSX.

In October 2021, the government issued a decree on the role and function of the MOF, which has led to the establishment of the Public Debt Management Department. This new department's functions include planning and evaluation, loan and guarantee management, loan project supervision, and overall public debt management.

5.2 Categories of the Lao PDR Government Securities

Article 19 of Law on Public Debt Management stipulates five categories of the government securities: Treasury Bill, Budget-Balancing Bond, Development Bond, Recapitalization Bond, and other types of bond such as Arrears-Clearance Bond (Table 3).

Table 3: Categories of Government Bonds

Government Bonds	Currency	Tenure	Frequency of Issuance	Channel of Issuance	Form of Issuance	Listing on LSX
Treasury Bill	LAK	≤1Y	Semiweekly	BOL	Paper	No
	LAK	≤1Y	Semimonthly	Securities firms	Scripless	Yes
Budget-balancing Bond	LAK	≥3Y	Semimonthly	Securities firms	Scripless	Yes
	USD	≥1Y	Semimonthly	Securities firms	Scripless	Yes
Development Bond	LAK	≥1Y	Irregularly	Directly to investors	Paper	No
Recapitalization Bond	LAK	≥1Y	Irregularly	Directly to investors	Paper	No
Arrears-Clearance Bond	LAK	≥1Y	Irregularly	Directly to investors	Paper	No

BOL = Bank of Lao, LAK = Lao Kip, LSX = Lao Securities Exchange, Y = year.
Source: Author's schematization.

Treasury Bill is a debt instrument to mobilize funds to finance the treasury's liquidity as per the public finance management plan of the MOF, with a payment term not exceeding 1 year. However, in recent years, the Bills have been issued mainly with a tenor of 1 year; thus, it is difficult to distinguish whether the Bills are issued for short-term liquidity management or to finance an annual budget. There are two issuance channels: one is offered to banks through the BOL, and the other is offered to various investors, including banks, through securities firms and agent banks.

Budget-Balancing Bonds or Fiscal Deficit Financing Bonds are a debt-type of financial instrument mobilizing funds to finance the annual fiscal deficit, with payment terms of at least 1 year. Budget-Balancing Bonds are issued through securities firms and agent banks and listed on the LSX. By 2020, Treasury Bills and Budget-Balancing Bonds were the major sources to finance the annual budget deficit domestically.

Development Bond or Investment Bond is a debt-type of financial instrument to mobilize funds to finance the implementation of infrastructure development projects, with a payment term in line with the return-on-investment period. Development Bond is issued directly to investors.

Recapitalization Bond is a debt-type of financial instrument to mobilize funds to recapitalize a state-owned enterprise, and a state-owned commercial bank aiming at improving liquidity and strengthening their finance structures, with a payment term in line with the state's periodic budget. Recapitalization Bond is issued directly to investors.

In case of emergency, the government may issue other types of bonds to address its liquidity issue and economic management as per the National Assembly's approved public debt ratio. Based on this, Arrears-Clearance Bond or Triangle Bond is issued. This bond involves three parties, namely, the government including the provinces, contractors keeping claims against the government, and commercial banks lending to the contractors. The government issues Arrears-Clearance Bonds directly to commercial banks in exchange for loans to contractors. Though the issuance of Arrears-Clearance Bonds and Development Bonds should be exceptional, such bonds have been issued occasionally, most recently in 2021.

A notable characteristic of the Lao PDR government bond market is its high dependency on Treasury Bills and Arrears-Clearance Bonds (Table 4).

Table 4: Domestic Government Bonds Outstanding

Type of Debt	Type of Bonds	2019	2020	2021
Government bond	Investment bond (development bond)	729	446	10,442
	Arrears-Clearance Bond	2,887	2,714	6,885
	Budget-Balancing Bond (through LSX)	1,469	2,480	3,593
	Treasury bill (through BOL)	3,062	2,821	2,314
Total		**8,147**	**8,461**	**23,234**

BOL = Bank of Lao, LAK = Lao kip, LSX = Lao Securities Exchange, MOF = Ministry of Finance, PPG = public and publicly guaranteed.
Source: MOF, *Annual PPG Debt Statistics Bulletin*, annual series.

The composition of the government bonds implies weakness in debt and cash management. Due to insufficient data on revenue, expenditure, and cash position, the government may not be able to make a forecast of its expenditure and payment schedule. In addition, a lack of consolidating cash balance at the Treasury Single Account (TSA) would cause inefficient cash management. Therefore, the cash position needs to be maintained relatively high. Or, unexpected and unscheduled payments may have to be postponed, which would create a potential source of the Arrears-Clearance Bond. In other words, by improving the ability to collect data on the current state of debts, expenditures, and cash position holistically in a timely and accurate manner, the government may be able to improve its debt position.

In relation to debt management, sound government cash management should stabilize and minimize the government's cash balance, thus enabling the government to reduce the volume of debts and associated costs. In many countries, central banks carry out the cash management function because changes in the government's cash balance at the TSA directly impact the current account balance and level of required reserve of the banks at the central bank. Currently, a large share of government cash is held at commercial banks (Table 5). This size of deposits at commercial banks in comparison to the Treasury Bills implies the existence of idle cash and room for debt reduction.

Table 5: Government Deposits at Commercial Banks and the BOL
(LAK billion)

	2018	2019	2020	2021	2022 Q1
Commercial banks	1,600	2,305	2,305	3,624	4,578
BOL	938	1,908	1,336	1,897	2,497
Total	**2,537**	**4,212**	**3,641**	**5,520**	**7,075**

BOL = Bank of Lao, LAK = Lao kip, Q = quarter.

Note: Totals may not sum precisely because of rounding.

Source: BOL, "Money and Banking Statistics," monthly series.

5.3 Issuance Process of Government Securities in the Lao PDR

Most Treasury Bills are offered through the BOL to banks semiweekly. Treasury Bills are also offered through securities firms and agent banks, but their purchase is small because the nonbank investor base is still small in the Lao PDR. Budget-balancing Bonds are offered only through securities firms biweekly; thus, banks purchase the bonds through the securities firms. Since late 2021, the MOF has started the interest rate auction of Treasury Bills at the BOL. The bills and the bonds issued through securities firms are offered with a fixed coupon and price set by the MOF. Therefore, there may be a gap between the amount the MOF would like to issue and the amount investors would like to subscribe. This may create an unexpected shortage of funds if the amount subscribed is significantly lower than what the MOF would like to issue. There is no primary dealer in the Lao PDR at this stage; thus, there is no financial institution to act as a market maker of government securities.

Treasury Bills offered through the BOL are issued in paper form; thus, banks subscribed to the bills must collect the paper from the MOF. The Treasury Bills and Budget-Balancing Bonds offered through securities firms are listed on the LSX, thus, the bills and bonds are issued in scripless and deposited at the LSX.

To ensure smooth issuance and transactions of the government securities, it is desirable to consolidate the issuance and transaction channels. In other ASEAN markets, the government securities are issued through primary dealers

(Table 6) and deposited at the central banks or the central securities depository (CSD) in scripless or immobilized form; thus, transactions of the government bonds can be done electronically.

Primary dealers are appointed by the government or its issuing agency, i.e., a central bank, to bid for and absorb sovereign securities in the primary market, thereby ensuring full placement of individual issues and giving the government the certainty that the intended funding operation will be successful. The role of primary dealers carries obligations and privileges. Primary dealers need to ensure the smooth placement of the government securities. This may include an obligation to bid at an auction and underwrite a certain amount. In addition, primary dealers need to make a market; thus, they always need to show a price indication to buy and sell to create market liquidity (footnote 10).

Table 6: Primary Dealers in Selected ASEAN Member States

	Malaysia	Singapore	Thailand	Viet Nam
Banks	• AmBank • CIMB • Citibank • Hong Leong • HSBC • J.P. Morgan Chase • Maybank • OCBC • Public Bank • RHB • Standard Chartered Bank • UOB	• ANZ • Bank of America • Barclays • BNP Paribas • Citibank • Credit Suisse • DBS • Deutsche Bank • HSBC • Maybank • OCBC • Standard Chartered Bank • UOB	• Bangkok Bank • Bank of America • BNP Paribas • CIMB Thai Bank • Citibank • Deutche Bank • HSBC • J.P. Morgan Chase • Krungthai Bank • Kasikorn Bank • Siam Commercial Bank • Standard Chartered Bank • TMB Bank	• Agribank • Asia Commercial Bank • BIDV • HDBank • Maritime Bank • Military Bank • Orient Commercial Bank • Sacombank • Saigon Commercial Bank • Southeast Asia Bank • Techcombank • TPBank • Vietinbank • VPBank
Securities firms			• KGI Securities	• BIDV Securities • Hochiminh City Securities • Saigon Hanoi Securities • Vietcombank Securities
Source	Bank Negara Malaysia	Monetary Authority of Singapore	Bank of Thailand	Ministry of Finance, Viet Nam
Remark	Primary dealers for non-Islamic	Primary dealers for institutional investors	Primary dealers for outright transactions	Primary dealers for 2022

ANZ = The Australia and New Zealand Banking Group Limited, BIDV = Bank for Investment and Development of Vietnam, CIMB = Commerce International Merchant Bankers Berhad, DBS = Development Bank of Singapore Limited, HDBank = Ho Chi Minh City Development Joint Stock Commercial Bank, HSBC = Hongkong and Shanghai Banking Corporation, OCBC = Oversea-Chinese Banking Corp, TMB = TMBThanachart Bank Public Company Limited, UOB = United Overseas Bank Limited, VPBank = Vietnam Prosperity Joint Stock Commercial Bank.

Source: Author's schematization.

Currently, it is difficult to anticipate how much Treasury Bills and Budget-Balancing Bonds would be subscribed by banks and other investors. To conduct efficient and effective debt and cash management, it is desirable to have a good forecast of how much would be subscribed. To ensure successful government securities issuance, the Lao PDR may need to consider introducing primary dealers in the market. Good communication with primary dealers would support understanding of the market conditions and the appetite of investors.

5.4 Depository of Government Securities in the Lao PDR

In the Lao PDR, a large portion of the government securities are issued in paper form. This impedes efficient and safe transactions of the government securities, hence, reduces market liquidity and eventually leads to a higher cost of issuance. In ASEAN markets, government securities are deposited at the central banks or CSD (Table 7).

Table 7: Government Securities Depository in Selected ASEAN Member States

Central bank (including its subsidiary)	Indonesia, Malaysia, Singapore
Central Securities Depository	Indonesia, Thailand

Source: Author's schematization.

Central banks often function as a depository for government securities, because they need to execute a monetary policy through open market operations with such securities. Disruptions in securities depository operations directly affect monetary operations. In addition, it is operationally easier to manage delivery-versus-payment (DVP) of cash and securities in a real-time gross settlement (RTGS) system under the central bank. Having both the securities depository and cash (RTGS) legs under one platform facilitates settlement automation and operational risk management. Functions of securities depository are essential for the timely posting or delivery of collateral for payments, development of the capital market, and other liquidity management. The central bank's intraday credit, either for monetary policy or payment systems purposes, depends heavily on the timely availability of collateral, for which government bonds are deemed the preferable assets. Because the government bonds are often considered almost equivalent to cash, central banks may prefer to function as a securities depository of government securities (footnote 10).

5.5 Pricing of Government Securities at the Primary Market

In the Lao PDR, at the time of each issuance through securities firms, the MOF sets a coupon rate and sells at par only, not through a competitive price bidding. There is no room for auction participants to negotiate the price of the bond.

The MOF seems to set a coupon rate or price with reference to deposit rates (Tables 8 and 9). Given the early stage of market development, it is understandable for the MOF to wish to control the coupon rate and price of government securities. However, this would create uncertainty in funding. It is very difficult to anticipate how much can be raised through the auction. Therefore, each issuance may result in too much cash or too little, compared to the required funding.

Table 8: Interest Rates of Treasury Bill and Budget-Balancing Bond

Product	Currency	1Y	2Y	3Y	5Y	7Y	10Y	15Y	20Y
Treasury bill	LAK	5.00%							
Budget-balancing bond	LAK			6.80%	6.95%	7.20%	7.50%	7.70%	8.00%
	USD	5.00%	5.50%	6.00%	7.00%	7.50%	8.00%		

LAK = Lao kip, MOF = Ministry of Finance, USD = United States dollar, Y = year.
Source: MOF, *Prospectus*, Mar 2022.

Table 9: Average Deposit Rates in Commercial Banks (Mar 2022)

Currency	Savings	Fixed deposit				
		1Y	2Y	3Y	4Y	5Y
LAK	1.68%	5.30%	6.20%	6.83%	6.89%	6.96%
USD	1.09%	3.71%	4.92%	5.94%	6.65%	6.76%

LAK = Lao kip, USD = United States dollar, Y = year.
Source: BOL, "Money and Banking Statistics," monthly series.

Meanwhile, the MOF has started the interest rate auction of Treasury Bills at the BOL since late 2021. It takes the form of a multiple price auction. The BOL announces the winning rate in weighted average, and the volume, on its platform.

In general, there are three issuance methods of government securities. A competitive auction is most useful and desirable to create a market. A syndicated underwriting is useful for distributing widely and creating a broad investor base, including small financial institutions. A private placement can be negotiated, for example, to place long-term bonds to a small number of expected investors such as pension funds and life insurance companies.

These three methods are not exclusive; a government can consider an appropriate issuance method along with market conditions and may combine the methods if necessary. But in principle, it is desirable to gradually shift to a competitive auction and for the MOF to act as a price-taker. This may raise concern about increasing the cost of issuance at the beginning, but it will ensure the reliability of market-determined yield or price, which will attract more investors to the market, hence, eventually reduce the cost of issuance.

5.6 Secondary Market

As there is no reporting on physical transfers of Treasury Bills, it is difficult to capture a comprehensive picture of secondary market transactions. But there were no transactions over the past several years between the BOL and commercial banks except the purchase of Arrears-Clearance Bonds from banks since 2019. As a part of open market operations, the BOL offers repo and collateralized lending facilities to commercial banks; however, they have not been utilized. The Treasury Bills and Budget-Balancing Bonds issued through securities firms have been listed on the LSX since December 2018. But there have been few transactions since then. There would be various reasons behind the lack of a secondary transaction, but to start the market, it is necessary to create enabling conditions for the central bank's market operations. Normally, government securities are recognized as high-quality assets to be used for the central bank's money market operations. Market operations such as repo and collateralized lending can be a starting point of the secondary market. Then, interbank transactions can be developed by following the central bank transactions. To facilitate market operations, infrastructure for monitoring market conditions, commercial banks' cash balances, and the Treasury Single Account, all need to be developed. In addition, much safer and more efficient payment and settlement systems for government securities need to be established, especially to attract foreign investors.

5.7 Investor Base

Unlike equities, bond market investors are mostly institutions. In emerging markets, banks tend to form a core group of investors in the government securities market in addition to their role as intermediaries and custodians of these instruments. Since the Lao PDR financial market is still at the early stage of development, banks are the most prominent investors of government securities.

Most government securities are held by commercial banks. Besides, approximately a quarter of them is held by Banque pour le Commerce Exterieur Lao Public (BCEL). In addition, the MOF issued Arrears-Clearance bonds in 2018 and 2021, and the BOL bought it from commercial banks since 2019. Hence, there is a skewed distribution of government securities in the market (Table 10).

Table 10: Credit to the Government by Commercial Banks and the BOL
(LAK billion)

	2018	2019	2020	2021	2022 Q1
Commercial banks	7,781	6,052	8,761	20,000	18,276
of which, govt held by BCEL	3,561	3,375	3,899	5,357	5,302
BOL	1,344	2,747	2,509	5,026	5,450
Total	**9,125**	**8,799**	**11,271**	**25,026**	**23,726**

BCEL = Banque pour le Commerce Exterieur Lao Public, BOL = Bank of Lao, Q = quarter.

Note: Totals may not sum precisely because of rounding.

Source: BOL, "Money and Banking Statistics," monthly series and BCEL financial statements.

Unlike the other countries, the share of institutional investors, such as the Lao Social Security Organization and the Deposit Protection Fund is not so large. Individual investors can subscribe the government securities through securities firms, and their share is 13.6% of government securities listed on the LSX as of the end of 2021.

Establishing a liquid and efficient bond market requires a broad and diverse investor base with different investment time horizons, risk appetites, and trading motives. A heterogeneous investor base is critical for enabling both the government and the corporate sector to execute their funding strategies under a wide range of market conditions. At the same time, a diverse investor base with different investment motives and time horizons stabilizes demand for bonds across various maturities. Hence, it is important that the bond market and various types of debt securities be accessible to many different groups of investors, including foreign investors.

5.8 Market Infrastructure for Cash and Securities Settlement

Mitigating settlement risk is critically important for government bond transactions because transaction values and volumes are significantly high, compared to other financial products. One of the most effective measures to reduce settlement risk is delivery-versus-payment (DVP). Therefore, a market infrastructure to ensure DVP in government bond transactions is a critical piece of the market development. In the Lao PDR, cash payments for Treasury Bills issued through the BOL are executed through the BOL accounts, transferring funds between commercial banks' accounts or between a commercial bank's account and the treasury account at the BOL. But the bills are issued in paper form by the MOF; thus, transactions of the bills must be delivered physically. This means it is very difficult to settle in DVP (Figure 3).

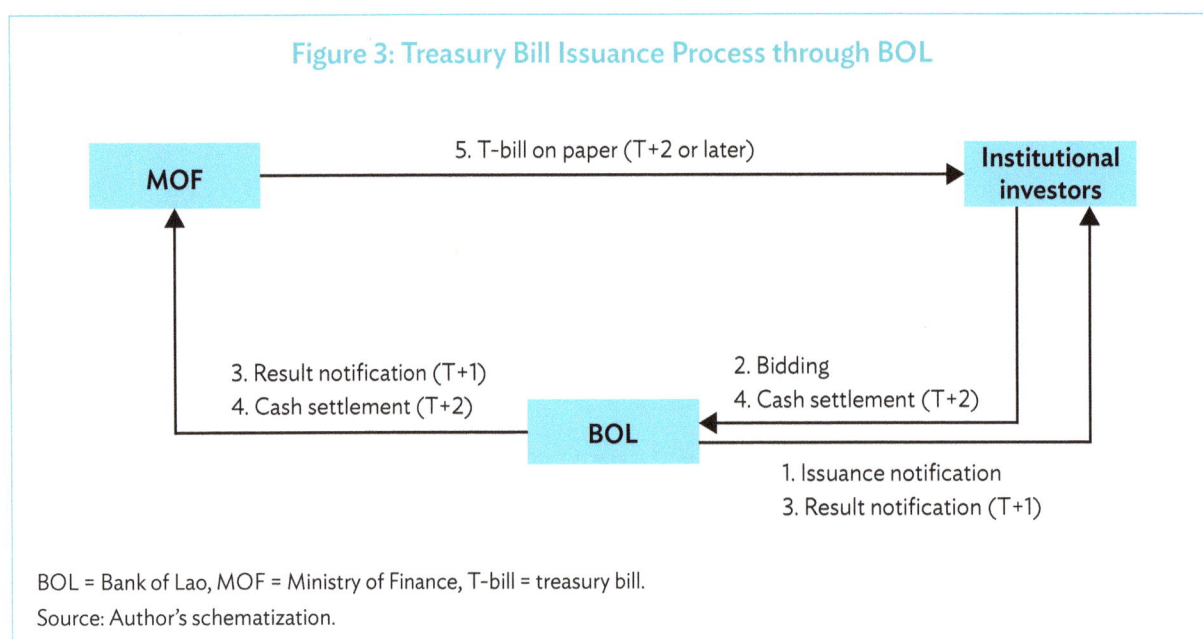

Figure 3: Treasury Bill Issuance Process through BOL

MOF

5. T-bill on paper (T+2 or later) → **Institutional investors**

3. Result notification (T+1)
4. Cash settlement (T+2)

2. Bidding
4. Cash settlement (T+2)

BOL

1. Issuance notification
3. Result notification (T+1)

BOL = Bank of Lao, MOF = Ministry of Finance, T-bill = treasury bill.
Source: Author's schematization.

Budget-balancing Bonds and Treasury Bills issued through securities firms are listed on the LSX; thus, they are transferable through securities accounts at the LSX. But LSX members are limited to securities firms. Hence, banks need to settle through the securities firms' accounts as their clients. Besides, a cash settlement of the bonds and bills is done through LSX settlement banks, namely BCEL and Lao Development Bank.[11] In addition, a buyer of the bonds and bills needs to keep funds in subscription accounts prior to the trade. Therefore, it is also very difficult to settle in DVP.

---

[11]   At the time of issuance, the cash settlement bank is limited only to BCEL.

Figure 4: Process of Budget-Balancing Bond Issuance through Securities Market

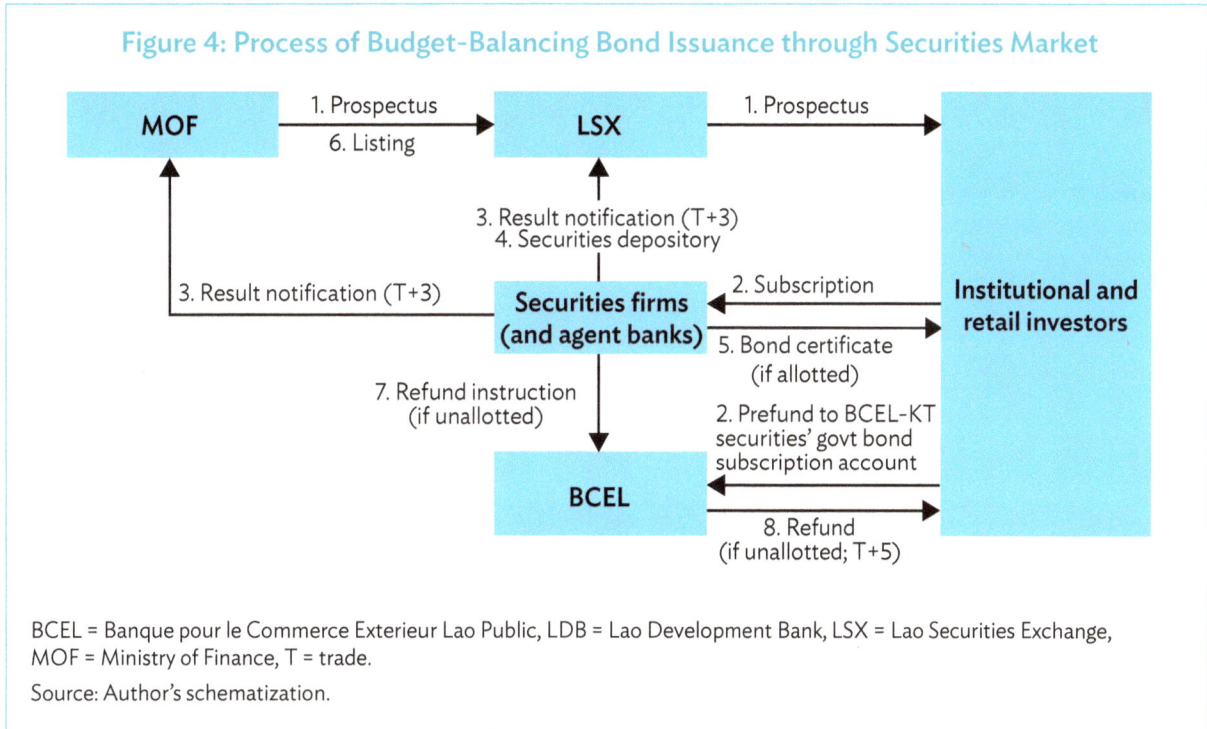

BCEL = Banque pour le Commerce Exterieur Lao Public, LDB = Lao Development Bank, LSX = Lao Securities Exchange, MOF = Ministry of Finance, T = trade.

Source: Author's schematization.

According to the Committee on Payment and Settlement Systems (CPSS), currently renamed to Committee on Payment and Market Infrastructure, DVP models are defined as follows:[12]

DVP model 1: A securities settlement mechanism that links a securities transfer and a funds transfer in such a way as to ensure that delivery occurs if and only if the corresponding payment occurs. DVP model 1 typically settles securities and funds on a gross and obligation-by-obligation basis, with the final (irrevocable and unconditional) transfer of securities from the seller to the buyer (delivery) if and only if the final transfer of funds from the buyer to the seller (payment) occurs.

DVP model 2: A securities settlement mechanism that links a securities transfer and a funds transfer in such a way as to ensure that delivery occurs if and only if the corresponding payment occurs. DVP model 2 typically settles securities on a gross basis, with the final transfer of securities from the seller to the buyer occurring throughout the processing cycle, but settles funds on a net basis, with the final transfer of funds from the buyer to the seller occurring at the end of the processing cycle

DVP model 3: A securities settlement mechanism that links a securities transfer and a funds transfer in such a way as to ensure that delivery occurs if and only if the corresponding payment occurs. DVP model 3 typically settles both securities and funds on a net basis, with final transfers of both securities and funds occurring at the end of the processing cycle.

The Lao PDR needs to consider introducing DVP in government securities transactions. Like the other countries, the Law on Payment System defines the BOL as the operator of the RTGS. Therefore, the cash settlement of government securities should be executed via the BOL RTGS.

---

[12]   CPSS. 2016. A glossary of terms used in payments and settlement systems. Basel.

6 Essential Building Blocks and Ecosystems to Develop the Lao PDR Government Bond Market

Based on the analysis in Section 5, the Lao PDR may prioritize developing the following building blocks and ecosystems.

6.1 Development of Sound Market Infrastructures

The Lao PDR needs to establish a sound securities settlement and safekeeping infrastructure to enable DVP. As a building block, it is necessary to establish a depository for the government securities that can connect with the central bank's RTGS and execute government securities transactions in DVP. There are two options to develop safe and efficient payment, clearing, and settlement systems in the Lao PDR.

First, the Lao PDR may consider establishing a new depository for the government securities separately from the LSX. The current system under the LSX is designed for equities transactions. But government securities transactions are inevitably large; thus, it is desirable to meet the requirement of DVP Model 1. Instructions for both securities and funds should be processed on a trade-by-trade basis, i.e., gross settlement, with the final and unconditional transfer of securities from the seller to the buyer occurring at the same time as the final transfer of funds from the buyer to the seller via the central bank system. The challenge would be the costs of developing new systems. Since cash and securities settlement systems in two different institutions must be connected and operated simultaneously, the systems would become more complicated.

Another option is to deposit all government securities at the BOL, and the BOL operates all transactions for the government securities. Once the securities in paper form are deposited at the BOL, it is not necessary to move the securities, i.e., immobilized; moreover, the securities can be issued in scripless. Since most government securities investors are banks, cash and securities settlement transactions can be executed smoothly through the BOL accounts. The BOL might need to develop a new system for depository recording, but since the operation of DVP can be performed in the same institution, delivery of cash and securities can be done more easily compared to linking systems in different institutions.

6.2 Enhancement of Treasury Single Account and Fiscal Information Disclosure

The Lao PDR needs to improve the availability of government bond information and market transparency. It is necessary to disclose its fiscal conditions, share its debt management policy and strategy, and announce an issuance schedule regularly in advance to market participants. But to do so, the government needs to improve cash management by enhancing the TSA and improving data collection related to revenue and expenditure. Sound cash management should stabilize and minimize the government's cash balance, thus enabling the government to reduce the volume of debts and associated costs. Besides, sound debt and cash management can catalyze broader financial market development and financial deepening.

Government debt and cash managers need to have an efficient information collection system. It is necessary to accurately project the volume and timing of the government's future cash inflows through tax, customs, and other revenues. Likewise, the volume and timing of outflows through salary payments, public expenditures, and the redemption of outstanding debt need to be estimated. Thus, future cash balances, including any seasonality, can be identified.

The information on past, current, and projected budgetary activities, including financing, and the consolidated financial position of the government, including short-term cash balances, should be publicly available in a timely manner. Effective communication and information sharing with the investor community are indispensable to developing the government bond market. This will eventually increase market confidence, leading to smoother, easier, and cheaper funding.

In this regard, it is worth noting that the MOF established the Public Debt Management Department effective 2022. It is expected that the department will improve its debt and cash management.

6.3 Introduction of Primary Dealers to Enhance Communication with the Market

The Lao PDR also needs to improve communication with market participants. In this regard, it is worth considering the introduction of primary dealers as a necessary building block. The primary dealership should be open to banks and securities firms.

Direct participants of government bond auctions are called primary dealers. Primary dealers are banks and securities firms that buy new issues directly from the government to resell them to investors, thereby acting as a market maker of government issues. Primary dealers are recognized based on capital resources, human resources, sales networks, and trading performance. The government may set a requirement such as the minimum amount of bidding and allocation by primary dealers. In turn, primary dealers may enjoy privileges such as exclusive bidding and underwriting rights and access to the central bank's standing cash borrowing arrangement.

Along with much closer communication with primary dealers, the MOF should develop the capacity to employ several issuance methods such as competitive auction, syndicated underwriting, and private placement. The MOF can begin with a single-price auction and then consider adopting a multiple-price auction for market participants to gain experience in bidding. Auctions should move to competitive bidding as institutional investors expand and primary market participants gain experience.

6.4 Expanding Investor Base

Usually, pension funds, provident funds, and insurance companies are core investors in government securities. Since their liability is much longer than banks, their capacity to invest will be crucial for the successful issuance of long-term government securities.

The Lao PDR has the Lao Social Security Organization and Deposit Protection Fund, which can be good investors for the government securities. Further collaboration and coordination with these institutions should be explored to create an opportunity for long-term stable funding.

To attract individual investors to the government bond market, savings bonds and collective investment schemes may be considered in the future. Since many individuals do not have bank accounts, the direct offering of savings bonds through mobile phones can provide an investment opportunity if adequately designed.

6.5 Coordination and Collaboration among the Relevant Authorities and Stakeholders

Cooperation and coordination among the policy-making authorities should be enhanced to place the building blocks and establish the ecosystem. The MOF as the issuer of the government securities, the BOL as the agent of the government and the facilitator of government securities transactions through its market operations, the LSCO as the guardian of market integrity and functionality, and the insurance and contractual savings authorities should communicate and coordinate closely for market development.

To ensure coordination among stakeholders and market participants, the economies that have successfully developed a local currency bond market have often adopted a high-level interagency bond market committee, led by the policy-making authorities, to guide and coordinate the implementation of interdependent tasks. Some economies faced difficulties in forming an interagency committee due to their unique government structures and/or the central bank's status in relation to the government. But, even if a formal interagency committee is not possible, it is highly preferable to have an informal coordination mechanism to ensure close communication among them. A lack of coordination and conflict of leadership among the policy-making authorities often creates confusion and is likely to result in limited outcomes.

Since the Lao Securities Commission (LSC) comprises the finance minister, the BOL governor, and deputy ministers of relevant ministries, the LSC can play a more active role as a coordinating body for the government bond market development.

7 Conclusion

To ensure a smooth and early recovery from the COVID-19 pandemic, emerging economies need to enhance their capacity to mobilize their domestic resources. Creating an efficient local currency government bond market is essential to support a more resilient recovery.

Lessons from the Asian Bond Markets Initiative can be extended to economies with a less developed local currency bond market. Development of such a market requires a comprehensive approach—because its building blocks are interrelated, and their interactions are dynamic—so a deep understanding and thorough analysis of the market is necessary.

In common with many emerging markets, the Lao PDR faces challenges, such as the need for (i) a safer and more efficient payment and settlement system, (ii) better debt and cash management, (iii) development of long-term investors, and (iv) strong coordination among regulators and stakeholders. However, detailed prescriptions need to be tailor-made. The Lao PDR may have basic building blocks, but the functionality of each block is still limited. In particular, debt and cash management need to be improved. Consolidation of cash to the Treasury Single Account needs to be enhanced. In government securities transactions, delivery-versus-payment will be necessary, especially to attract foreign investors. We hope these analyses and recommendations will encourage the development of a local currency bond market in the Lao PDR.